TABLE OF CONTENTS

Introduction

When I (Melanie) was a young girl, my grandfather molested me. Actually, he was my step-grandfather, but he and my grandmother married when I was a baby, so he was the only grandfather I ever knew. He sexually molested me. Many times.

It didn't happen for a short period of time, but repeatedly over a period of years. It was a fearful and confusing situation that left me unsure about what to do. As is true with any young girl facing such a challenge, it affected me profoundly, even into my adult life.

I was in my early thirties and the wife of a pastor (Steve) when my mother called me one day to tell me that my grandfather was in the hospital and expected to die. My immediate response was that I was *thrilled*. Finally, this man was going to get what he deserved.

I was full of anger and hate for what he had done to me, but I didn't realize just how much until I received this call. My long-festering vindictiveness surprised me through a sudden outburst: "Good! He'll finally go to hell and get what he deserves!" Even as the words came out of my mouth, I felt startled by my spontaneous reaction to the news my mother was telling me.

How do you break free from something like that? I didn't want to feel that way, but that's the way it was. Until I heard myself speak those words, I didn't realize just how much I still carried the pain of his abuse with me. This book will describe how Jesus Christ set me free from that kind of hatred.

On the other hand, I (Steve) never have experienced that extreme sort of traumatic hurt in my life. I can only imagine what it must have been like for Melanie. I grew up in a safe and loving home, and never knew the kind of hurt she experienced. In fact, it would be easy to conclude that there has never been a need for me to extend forgiveness toward anybody. If I had come to that conclusion, however, it would have left me less than whole in my own life.

The truth is that we've all been hurt, and it doesn't have to be by something tragic, like what happened to Melanie. To be attacked by a ravenous wolf is a horrific experience compared to the sting of a wasp, but even though the comparison reveals a huge gap in intensity, that doesn't mean that the sting of a wasp doesn't hurt.

I use this illustration because I don't want you to make the mistake of thinking, just because you may not have been hurt in the huge way that Melanie was, that the wrong done to you by others in your own life is inconsequential. While a ravenous attack can bring devastating damage to a person, it's important to realize that situations that appear far less menacing can also sting in a way that requires attention, too.

When I was receiving training to share this message of grace many years ago, a part of the process involved my receiving personal counseling. I remember the day I sat in the counselor's office with tears streaming down my cheeks. My voice quivered and my heart raced because on my lap sat a yellow legal pad covered with detailed accounts of the ways in which people I'd known had wronged me.

None of it was monumental, especially compared to the kind of thing Melanie faced, but that's the point we want you to see. It doesn't have to be monumental to have a debilitating effect on your life. Things that may have seemed small at the time can end up having a major impact.

My childhood was relatively pain-free. As I sat in the counselor's office during my training, I looked at the list in my hand. I had written the names of my offenders on that paper, and was mentally reviewing the offenses they had committed against me. Having served as a local church pastor since I was nineteen, most of the names on my list were church members who had wronged me in various ways. For two weeks, I had mulled and grieved over that list, remembering and recording every painful memory that God brought to mind.

I hadn't thought of some of those people or the situations I'd had with them for a long time. I had long-ago forgotten the bitter taste of those offenses–at least consciously. But I was learning how the aftertaste from some hurts never really goes away until we properly deal with them. Like onions or garlic on a person's breath, the effect of my past hurts had lingered for far too long.

Large Hurts or Small, They All Affect Us

While my offenses were not serious compared to my wife's, they had caused me to become bitter in ways that affected me at a subliminal level. Others probably never would have seen it, but it was there, tainting my outlook on many things in many ways.

Melanie had suffered a terrible thing, a horrible offense against a young child. But the effect of past hurts had been the same on us both. (It caused us to develop protective coping mechanisms to ensure we wouldn't be hurt again. It's an independent way of living that results in trying to manage life by developing self-sufficient techniques. It's independent in the sense that we are leaning on our own ability to navigate through life, instead of relying on the Christ who indwells us. It's doing the best we know how to do, given the situation we've had to face.

The problem is that it doesn't work–not at the heart level, which is where it all really matters. We can fake it, and even go through life seeming to do okay, but the reality is that it needs to be resolved. It needs to be healed. Whether others can see it or not, we have an emotional limp in our walk until it is healed.

Developing coping mechanisms is the default setting for our reaction to painful actions against us by others. That's why it is important that we come to understand how to be free from our past hurts. Until we do, we won't ever be able to live with the carefree abandon our Creator intends to characterize our lifestyles.

Our Vision for Setting you Free

Melanie and I have written this book together in order to do a number of things that we believe are really important. First, through sharing our own journey of overcoming wrongs against us, we want to help others see the way to move beyond the effects of wrong that they have experienced in life. We have all experienced hurts and offenses throughout our lives, some horrendous like Melanie's while others, more mundane; some, long ago, while others are more recent or ongoing. Either way, they need to be dealt with if we are going to live a whole and healthy lifestyle.

Second, we want to give you a scriptural method for dealing with painful past events that we both learned and now teach. It is an exercise, a practice, a process that we have found very accessible, successful, and deeply healing. Most people we have shared this exercise with have affirmed its value in their own lives. The exercise is an expression of grace that you will find to help you in a way that you probably can't even imagine, right now.

We begin our journey toward healing in this book by first looking at the importance of owning the wrong done to us. So many people trivialize the wrong done to them, to their own detriment. We believe it is critical to acknowledge not just what has happened to us, but how its effect continues to ripple through our lives, sometimes buried and unconscious, nevertheless holding us back from our birthright to walk in grace and freedom. You can't see any problem solved until you first acknowledge that there is one.

Then we will discuss the most important key to recovering from the wrong things done to us in our lives. This will be very helpful because so many people have misunderstood what is necessary to move forward beyond hurt in a way that is healthy. We will discuss misunderstandings about what we do and don't need to know and do, to find wholeness. You may be surprised to learn that this approach isn't nearly so complicated as some think it has to be. Some who have had years of counseling and therapy have found freedom through this simple, biblical approach. It's a simple step with profound results.

The two of us believe that it is important to clearly understand what the Bible teaches about finding healing from our past hurts, before the practical work presented in the second half of the book can be done. We will use numerous scriptural references because, when it comes to this kind of healing, there is no greater authority on the subject than God!

Then, we will give you a straightforward explanation of the ways to apply the scriptural instructions to your own specific circumstances. This is the heart of the book, because we believe so deeply that you can, and should, find freedom in your own life from the hurts of those who have sinned against you.

Finally, because we know that those who have hurt us may still be in our lives, and because we understand that new pain may continue to rise up in us, and new offenses committed against us, we will explain the ways that you, too, can apply what the Bible teaches about how to act towards those who have hurt you or even continue to hurt you. We'll talk about how to relate in a healthy way to those who keep doing wrong in a way that simultaneously shows grace and yet draws boundaries, allowing you to preserve your own dignity and self-respect.

1

Own The Wrong

Admitting that we have been affected by the wrongs done to us in life is the first step for someone who wants to be free. It's normal to rationalize that we've moved beyond the situation and, since we are now functioning normally, that everything is okay. The reality, however, is that, until we recognize and own what has happened to us, we can't forgive it.

"Forgive it?" you may ask. That's right. (The key to getting past the effects of wrongs done to us is forgiveness.) You may immediately have a negative reaction to the very idea of forgiving those who have wronged you. That's okay, too. Admit feeling that way. Honesty is always the best thing. Better to feel it than to deny it.

As you move forward in this book, we believe that the Holy Spirit will help you with your feelings. Why would He have you reading this book, if He didn't plan to help you in that way? He knows how you feel, and He isn't intimidated or put off by your feelings. God will work with you where you are, so long as you'll be honest about where you are. So, even if you have negative emotions right now, that can be a good thing because it shows that you do know the person who hurt you owes you. (It's not possible to release a person from what he owes you if you don't even recognize the debt.)

Where Have You Been Hurt In Your Life?

The truth is, all of us have been hurt in our lives. Some of us were hurt as children. Some of us were hurt in our adolescence, and some, in our adult life. But we've all been hurt. Everybody has been rejected.

In his book, *Handbook to Happiness*, author Charles Solomon says, "those who have been rejected in subtle ways may have just as much emotional damage but be unaware of the source. (By rejection," he says, "I mean the absence of meaningful love. Being rejected doesn't mean that there's no love involved, but that, for one reason or another, it's not fulfilling or edifying love."[1])

I want you to think about your own life, as we start this study together. I challenge you to (pray and ask the Holy Spirit to show you the hurts that have come to you, in your own life, and how they have affected you.)

The wounds that have come to us affect us to the very core of our being. Sometimes they happen to us when we are small children, as in the case of Melanie. At that time in our lives, we don't have the ability to understand what's occurring, which makes it hard for us to respond in a healthy way.

---

[1] Charles R. Solomon. *Handbook to Happiness*. Revised updated edition. Carol Stream, IL: Tyndale House Publishers, Inc., 1 Nov. 1999.

What Unforgiveness Does to our Lives

Unfortunately, (through denial and unforgiveness, we become bound to the person who hurt us.) It's a negative attachment, to be sure, but it's there nonetheless. Without understanding the pathway out through owning the reality of the effects of our hurts and through forgiveness, the painful memory in our hearts and our minds won't be healed. In fact, it can't be healed.

We don't realize that, unless we forgive and release the offender, we're going to continue to hold onto the hurt, rejection, or betrayal. Either consciously or unconsciously, the pain will affect us. Maybe we will be angry. Sometimes, we become depressed. Possibly, we'll find ourselves reacting disproportionately to anything that triggers negative emotions within us.

We have known people who have harbored unforgiveness for years and years, sometimes even after the person who had hurt them had died. Maybe that's the case in your life. In some instances, even though the perpetrator has been dead for many years, the survivor is still tormented by what that person did to them.

(Unforgiveness is like a chain that enslaves you to the person who hurt you.) It binds you to the person and the event that assaulted you. (You will only be free from the whole thing through forgiveness. There is no other way.)

We want to help you, first, to honestly assess that painful connection to those past offenders. Suppressing what happened won't solve the problem. It will only make it worse, over time.

Melanie's Deep Wounding as a Child

Melanie's story is rich and valuable to understand on many levels. It began when her own grandfather violated her as a child. She wasn't raped, but was molested, and over a period of many years.

I (Melanie) will describe my personal journey into the depths of unforgiveness that resulted from being hurt by somebody I loved very much, someone whom I initially thought loved me, as well.

While it is a painful history to read, we believe that you will appreciate it because the story doesn't stop with the pain, but goes on to describe how I found freedom from the hurt that came to me at the hands of my grandfather.

I (Steve) will describe my story, as well, in part because we recognize that not all of us suffer the kind of traumatic events that Melanie experienced. For many of us, our hurts may seem smaller, less consequential, and maybe even subliminal. For some readers, the hurts came from Christian people who hurt us in the name of the church, as they did a pastor like myself. No matter how old or how small, these offenses are painful to us nonetheless.

We're going to look at these hurts, and write not just about ourselves but, more importantly, about Jesus. In the context of our experiences, we will explore the forgiveness that He has offered to all those who hurt Him, and through understanding that, we'll learn how to extend that same forgiveness to other people.

I (Melanie) was a little girl of about five or six when my abuse began. My grandfather was the one person in my life who gave me love and affection. I was a middle child, so I felt like I didn't get much attention from anybody, but my grandfather would come over and let me dance on his feet. He'd set me on his big shoes, hold my hands, and walk around the room as I danced. He'd sit me on his lap, and swing me around in his arms. I remember so many times just being held and cuddled by him. That was very important to me. I didn't get that kind of affection from anybody else.

But then the time came when that stopped being the kind of attention he gave me. Although I felt very safe with him in the beginning, I came to realize that he didn't necessarily love me because of who I was. He wanted to be around me because of *what* I was–I was a little child, and he was a child molester.

That is what child molesters do. They want to be around young children so they can gain their trust, then they begin to abuse them in whatever way they choose.

Once they've gained a child's trust, it becomes easy to do that.

I was hungry to experience love, just like we all are. We are all born with the three basic needs: to be loved, valued, and accepted. I did feel that love from my grandfather, but soon learned that it was not real love. It was a distortion, a perversion–something evil and very wrong. As much as I wanted to believe that he loved me in an appropriate way, the time came when I couldn't deny it anymore. Something was seriously wrong.

When I spent the night with my grandparents, after everybody else had gone to sleep, my grandfather came into the living room where I slept on the foldout couch. I could hear him coming down the hall. I felt afraid. I knew why he was coming into the room.

I remember very vividly hearing, as he came towards me, his unzipping his pants as he walked. He would come and sit on the edge of the bed where I was supposed to be asleep. I would pretend to be asleep as he proceeded to have me sit up and fondle him. It would proceed from there.

This kept on until I was thirteen. As the years went on, and as this continued to happen, I developed feelings about what was going on.

As a small girl, I instinctively knew that what he was doing wasn't right, but it was confusing. On the one hand, he was very affectionate, and I liked that. On the other, I didn't like what he did by molesting me. My young mind was too immature to sort it out and make sense of it.

As I got older, I began to understand that this wasn't right. I told some of my friends what was going on. They told me that I needed to tell my parents. But I thought that my parents wouldn't believe me, if I told them, so I just kept quiet.

Finally, though, the day came when I did tell my grandfather that, if he didn't stop, I was going to tell. He just laughed and said that they weren't going to believe me. He confirmed the underlying fear I already had.

The worst part came in the betrayal that I felt. I had loved him so much, and he betrayed that love. When children love somebody, they do it without reservation. It was very difficult for me to deal with the fact, in years afterwards, that someone could betray the heart of a child in that way.

We both realize that this description of what happened to Melanie as a child is somewhat graphic, but we believe that it's important to share it with you, openly, because it allows you to understand the kind of trauma that was inflicted on her. What she went through has also happened to many other people.

Melanie shares in detail for another reason, as well. When you hear the story of how God brought her to a place of forgiveness, you will truly be able to understand the magnitude of that miracle. We trust it will generate faith in you about your own situation.

"Flesh": The Pain of Unforgiveness

There is a gnawing ache that comes from unforgiveness. When we don't fully recognize our pain or know how to yield it to Jesus Christ, what we do is develop ways to get around it–ways to cope and move forward with life, despite what has happened to us.

The biblical word for it is "flesh." It's the way we try to get our own needs met when we're not depending on the sufficiency of Jesus Christ. Sometimes we just don't know better. Make no mistake about it–a "flesh walk" is a dead-end journey. (God wants more for us than that we simply cope with our hurts. He wants to show us how He has conquered those hurts, and wants to enable us to rise above them and live in emotional, mental, and spiritual wholeness.)

All of us have flesh patterns. (The reality is that the offenses that have been committed against you in your life have caused you to develop certain methods, certain techniques, certain strategies to try and find acceptance from people, and from yourself.)The reason we know that is true is because it is a universal experience.

We all have developed these coping mechanisms, but flesh patterns are like fingerprints. No two of us have the same exact kind of flesh. Nonetheless, we all have the patterns. We all want to be loved. We all want to be accepted. Until we learn better, we will do whatever it takes to get that love and acceptance.

In my (Melanie) case, I began to develop patterns of trying to be a pleaser. I was living out of my people-pleaser flesh pattern, and was trying to cause others to like me. To an extent, it seemed to work.

I was on the Homecoming Court in high school and had many good friends. People affirmed me, but in my heart of hearts, I didn't feel like any of it was true. That low self-esteem followed me long into my adult life.

I (Steve) started dating Melanie when she was fifteen years old. She didn't know how pretty she was. She didn't know how popular she was. It took me a long time to understand how she could be so blind to what others so clearly saw. Why couldn't she see herself the way the rest of us saw her? It was because she had embraced the offense that had been committed against her, and it was festering inside of her. As a young girl who felt contaminated, how *could* she see herself objectively? Her grandfather had stolen that ability away from her the first time he touched her.

Time Doesn't Heal All Wounds: Owning your Painful Past

Melanie endured her grandfather's offense against her as a child. She grew to be a popular teenager and an adult woman who is beautiful in every way, but time doesn't heal all wounds. Her personal hurt came into full view that day her mother called her with news that her grandfather was gravely ill.

I (Melanie) was about 33 years old when my mother called to tell me that he was in the hospital, and not expected to live. I had no idea of the depth of the hatred and the anger that I had against him. As I shared earlier, I was so excited by the thought that this man would leave this world and go straight to hell.

The truth is, though, that the *real* Melanie would never feel that way. The impulsive explosion of angry passion about his death was another eruption of pain coming from deep inside me. The next thing that hit me was, "Wow, you have *that much hatred* towards someone?"

I didn't know it was there. I never knew, in fact, until the moment when I was faced with the thought that he might truly die. I was amazed at the depth of my emotions.

When Melanie was faced with the reality that her grandfather might die, she was stunned to recognize how deep her negative feelings still ran. Sometimes, when people hurt us, we suppress or even repress the memory of that offense against us. It still has an effect on us, whether we're conscious of it or not. That's why we must own it if we truly want to move completely past it.

Think about your own life for a moment. What has happened to you in life that has shaped the way you have learned to cope? What has happened that has caused you to react to the world around you in the ways that you do? Make no mistake about it, past hurts affect us in our soul, (mind, will and emotions), and (when our soul is contaminated with unforgiveness, there is an underlying anger there that's going to interfere with our capacity to live our lives the way God intends.)

In order to heal it, in order to remove the interferences, you first have to know that the anger is there. Don't think for a minute that the effect of past hurts in your life has diminished over the years. (Don't believe the lie that, just because you don't consciously think of it day after day, its effect doesn't still impact you every day. You may have absorbed it and learned to walk forward despite what has happened, but apart from forgiveness, you will walk with a limp whether you know it or not.)

In their book *Happiness is a Choice*, authors Frank Minirth and Paul Meier say this:

> Anger is hard to deal with unless an individual realizes it is there. If he becomes angry out of proportion with the actual event, it

may be because the event reminded him of another period in his life when he felt inferior and inadequate. (The current event reinforces those past feelings and insecurities. Perhaps 25% of his response was to the current situation, and the other 75% was to feelings that were long ago repressed.[2])

Things that happened to us in the past affect us, today. Maybe you're conscious of those things. However, many of us are not. We are laying this out before you as something for you to pray about and consider.

Could it be that the barrier that prevents you from moving forward and living the life you sense you were created to live is *unforgiveness*? Do you own the reality of the wrongs done to you? You can't forgive until you do.

---

[2] Frank B. Minrith and Paul D. Meier. *Happiness is a Choice.* Grand Rapids, MI: Baker Books, 2007.

Anger & Unforgiveness are Roadblocks to a Full Life

As I (Steve) have counseled people over the past forty years, I have often seen that, when people experience a roadblock to enjoying life but aren't able to put their finger on what that roadblock is, the answer is often an issue of unforgiveness. (It is a hidden weight in their psyche that most definitely hinders them, but they don't even know it is there.)

I have been sharing the message of who we are in Christ since 1990. Through the years, it has been very common for people to say to me: "Steve, I understand it, in my head. I know what you're saying. I can speak the language. I understand the theology, the doctrine of it. It makes sense. But how do I get this teaching from my head to my heart?"

I understand what they're asking. What they mean is, "How do I come to the place where the reality of Christ in my life is experiential, and not just a doctrinal truth that I recognize is real at an intellectual level?"

I have found that, when I discuss this with people one-on-one, the thing that has often prevented them from being able to appropriate the reality of Christ in their lives is the fact that there is unforgiveness in their hearts. They sincerely want to live the life they know they were created to live, but simply can't do it. It isn't uncommon that, once I have walked them through what you will learn in this book, they experience major breakthroughs in their lives.

It's Not the Severity: It's the Perception of Our Wounds

Melanie's offense was a traumatic one. My offenses were more ordinary, but they affected me, nonetheless. Because they were so ordinary, it was easy for me to not really own them, or see the effect they had on me. That's never good.

I mentioned my story about sitting in my counselor's office, and how I brought up those things that I had suppressed for many, many years. In fact, I had repressed some hurts until they had become unconscious memories, but still, an unexplained sourness deep down inside of me remained, an inner tension, because I had not forgiven people who needed to be forgiven.

God used a counselor to bring me to a place where I saw my own flesh in light of the hurts that I had experienced. It was through his counsel that I came to see the effects of unforgiveness in my own life. That's what we are praying will happen with you.

At the time I went through the experience of seeing and owning my past and rooting out unforgiveness, I had been a pastor for almost 21 years. I certainly didn't see myself as a martyr in any sense of the word. In fact, if some people were to look at my list detailing how I'd been hurt, they might even dismiss it as inconsequential. It's possible that they would say, "Not that much has happened to you. A lot of people have been hurt worse than you were."

What is important to understand, however, is that this book presents you with examples from both ends of the spectrum. The offense Melanie describes was traumatic. Mine were ordinary. What we want to show is that it isn't the severity of the offense against a person that creates the hurt. It's how they perceive that situation. We will keep repeating this concept throughout the book because we want to emphasize it.

All of us have experienced pain in our lives to some extent. For some of us, it was intentionally inflicted upon us. For others, it might have been purely unintentional, but the bottom line is this: when we fail to own what has happened and fail to understand the way to properly resolve those things, problems are going to arise, and there is a direct correlation between those problems and the denial and unforgiveness that may hold us, currently.

We All Try to Do our Best by Internalizing

To try to cope with painful events in the best way that we know how is normal. We try to function in a normal, acceptable way. Many people deal with their pain by internalizing it, and then, what they call "getting on with life." In most cases, with the passing of time, a person's awareness of the pain does subside. They might think that the situation is all over, and it might be accurate to say that the situation, itself, is over. It would be far from true to suggest that the *effect* of the painful event has passed, however.

(Unresolved pain that has been internalized has an accumulative effect on you. I (Steve) came to realize that I'd spent most of my life internalizing pain that I had experienced along the way. I assumed that, because I was able to cope with it and move beyond it, everything was okay.)

When I was a child, I internalized injustices that I perceived because there is usually no viable outlet to do anything else. I was still young. Then, I became a local church pastor at 19 years old, and served in that capacity for over 20 years. Pastors have very few options for venting their frustrations over personal insults.

I don't know if you realize this or not—if you're a pastor, you do; if you're not, you may not know this: there are bullies in the church!(There are people in the church world that will say things to a pastor that they'd never say to anybody else,)because anybody else would deck them for some of the things that they say.

They know that a pastor's role normally necessitates a certain level of restraint in his response. Since he often won't respond, some people know they'll get by with saying harsh things to him. While there are some who will push back, most pastors simply internalize those painful encounters.

Tim LaHaye hit it on the head in his book, *Anger is a Choice*.[3] This so describes the way that I was:

> I can keep up the image. I can smile. I can act friendly. I can hide the fact that I really don't forget. But, deep inside me is the burning fire of memory. (We've all learned to cover and hide our hurts, disappointments and anger. Eventually, however, the hurts, disappointments and anger will surface.)

Then LaHaye writes this story:

> I'm reminded of a story of a minister and a deacon playing golf. Both were having a terrible time. Every time that the deacon's ball went into the rough or off course, he'd swear. But when the minister's ball went into the sand pit or into

---

[3] Tim LaHaye. *Anger is a Choice*. Grand Rapids, MI: Zondervan Publishers, 2002.

the water, he'd just smile and say nothing. Finally, the deacon said, 'That's what I appreciate about you. When your ball goes off the fairway or into the water, you just smile.' 'That may be true,' said the minister. 'But where I spit, the grass dies!'

As a former local church pastor, I can tell you that I relate to that story. I, too, found that, in my own life, I had gradually come to the point where the grass died wherever I spit. And I'd spit at times when it didn't even make sense, not even to me.

Maybe I'd spit an insult at a driver in another car who drove too slowly when I wanted to get down the road. Or maybe I'd spit a harsh word at my young children when they left the refrigerator door open. I might even spit at myself when I forgot something that I meant to take with me to the office.

The point is, my reactions were seldom severe, but they were often inappropriate to the situation that I was facing. I don't think that even my own family would say that I was a short-tempered person, but I could have been called *tense*. And that tension was the result of unresolved pain that was caused by suppressed hurts.⊃ The pain had unconsciously accumulated over the years.

What are Your Traumas & Wounds That Deny your Authentic Self?

Has that happened in your life? Maybe you've had trauma, like Melanie, or something of that nature. Maybe it was a divorce, a bitter divorce. Maybe you were molested. Or maybe you had someone unfairly fire you from a job. Perhaps a friend betrayed you in some way.

What was it? Maybe it wasn't traumatic, and perhaps by comparison it almost seems trivial, and yet those offenses against you were still hurtful, deep down.

One of the things that keep us in emotional and spiritual bondage is to compare ourselves to others. Those of us who have had ordinary rejection and hurts sometimes compare ourselves to those, like Melanie, who've had really traumatic hurts in life. As a result, we tend to trivialize what has happened to us. We may say, "Oh, it's no big deal …" We'll discuss this further in a later chapter.

You need to know that, whenever you've been hurt, it *is* a big deal, and you've developed flesh patterns (coping mechanisms) around those hurts. (These flesh patterns are walls that we build up to protect ourselves. We construct protective barriers around ourselves to keep from being hurt. To the extent we do that, we begin to depend on our coping mechanism, walking after the flesh, and we stop living as our authentic self, as the child of God that we are.)

We fail to live out of our true identity. We put on a "flesh mask," and we live as a caricature of our real selves. In doing so, we are robbed of the opportunity to share our true selves with others.

Wearing the "flesh mask"

When I was a pastor who walked after the flesh and didn't know my identity in Christ–my authentic self–I wore a mask. It wasn't intentional, but I wore it all the time. I don't mean I acted one way at church and a different way at home. I didn't do that. I continuously wore the "pastor mask." I put my energy into projecting the person who I thought I ought to be. I wore that mask so long that, as a pastor, when I looked in the mirror, that's the person I saw. I didn't even know the real me.

I once told my counselor, "I know who I am in Christ. What I don't know is, who I am in this world. Because I've been 'the reverend' for so long, 'the pastor' for so long–I don't know how to function as a normal person. I don't know who I am in this world." I had lived behind the mask for so long, I didn't even know my authentic self.

What mask do you live behind? Do you hide the real you? In what ways have you learned to cope? If what you're doing is coping, you can be assured there is hurt inside you. Are there things that you've never addressed? Are there issues that you've never dealt with? Own it.

After Recognition, Forgiveness ... *REALLY!?*

The only way that you're going to experience the life you are meant to live is by allowing the Holy Spirit to bring up these areas where there needs to be forgiveness, and then appropriating that forgiveness. The gnawing ache of unforgiveness finds its roots deep down inside us, even when nobody knows. (Only God's Spirit can show that to you and then do something about it.)

(The only portal to freedom is through extending forgiveness toward the offender.) A statement like that may raise some initial objections in your mind. It may also provoke quite a few questions. Things like, "Yeah, but what about ..." and "Oh, but you don't know ..."

I (Melanie) am living proof that, regardless of the type of offense that's been committed against you, (there is grace in Jesus Christ to empower you to forgive the people who have done you wrong.)

I don't know what your circumstance is, but I encourage you, as you go forward in reading this book to (open your heart and mind in a way that will allow the Holy Spirit to speak to you, and to set you free.)

Wouldn't it be wonderful if you could have absolute freedom from your past? Wouldn't it be wonderful if you found yourself being elevated and promoted to a new, higher level of living? What if your life was brought a new joy, a new peace? What if you could experience the "peace that passes understanding," as described in the Bible?

You can. The key to all of that is in forgiving. We realize that many people have been so wounded that the very idea of forgiveness causes them to become angry. The enemy of their souls can bring up a lot of objections in their minds. But we truly believe that (forgiveness is the doorway to a free life.)

As ones who know our identity in Christ, we understand that forgiveness is that last hurdle that we must cross, by the power of the Holy Spirit, in order to enjoy and experience all that God has for us.

Now that we have examined the importance of owning the wrongs done to us, we can move forward to examine *why* it is possible to forgive, even though it may seem impossible right now.

♦ ♦ ♦
♦ ♦ ♦

2

Forgive the Unforgivable

Once we have owned the offense committed against us, it becomes possible to forgive the one who did wrong to us. Don't read assumptions into that statement. We aren't saying that you will necessarily need to reestablish a relationship to the person whom you forgive. For that matter, you may not even need to see or talk to them. As you'll see in this chapter, *forgiveness is a unilateral act* on the part of the one who extends it. It may or may not involve interaction with the other person. That all depends on the situation. For now, keep an open mind because no two hurtful situations are exactly the same.

Bitterness Blocks our River of Life

Unforgiveness produces a gnawing, emotional effect in our lives, whether the offense that was committed was traumatic in nature, like the one that Melanie experienced, or if it seems to be more minor, like what Steve experienced in the pastorate. Either way, the offense hurts, and it affects you.

The only way that we're going to be free to really walk in our identity in Christ and be true to our authentic self is to appropriately deal with the matter of unforgiveness in our hearts. We hope that you already see and believe this. It's an important first step toward freedom.

As she explained, Melanie was molested as a young child and, being so young, didn't understand what was going on for a number of years. Ultimately, the day came when she reached a level of maturity and realized that what her grandfather was doing was a horrible thing. After that, although the offensive behavior stopped, Melanie began to develop feelings of bitterness, contempt, and even hatred towards her grandfather.

Unforgiveness is like filth down in an artesian well. An artesian well is the spring that springs forth from underground, and if there is blockage down in that well, the water can't flow out in an unrestricted way. It may seep out around the filth, but even then, the water that escapes will be polluted. In order for that artesian well to spring forth with pure water again, the filth down in there–the blockage–has to be flushed out of it. Sometimes what erupts is a smelly, stinking mess.

That's how it is with unforgiveness. Sometimes the things in our lives related to past hurts have been suppressed so that the River of Life, that river of living water that Jesus said would spring from our innermost being, finds itself impeded by the barrier of unforgiveness in our hearts.

That's not to suggest that we can't see God at work in our lives at all. God's grace is bigger than our hurts. We certainly can still see that Jesus expressing Himself in our lives at certain times and in certain ways. However, in our heart of hearts, we know that we're not fully experiencing the kind of life that God intends. (The only way that we're going to experience that freedom, and the only way that that river of living water is going to flow forth from us in the way that God wants, is by washing out all of that suppressed or repressed unforgiveness down in our hearts.)

The Holy Spirit Brings Unforgiveness out of Hiding

If He brings the unforgiveness out of the hidden place inside us and causes us to see it, then it can be dealt with properly and appropriately. (When something surfaces into your consciousness from deep within you, recognize that as the work of the Holy Spirit.) You never would have seen it if it weren't for Him at work in you. He is bringing things to mind so that they (can be dealt with and disposed of) and so that those issues won't have power over you anymore.

Just like garbage in a well can pollute the water, in the same way, (unforgiveness in your heart towards other people can pollute your whole life.) It can keep you from enjoying all that God has for you.

We tend to think, as I (Steve) did in my own life, that if we just put it to the side, and then continue go forward without thinking about it, then everything will be okay. ("If I don't focus on it, then surely I'll get past it and I will function normally." That kind of thinking is a trap. It causes us to think to ourselves that there's no real need to forgive because, after all, it doesn't affect me at all now. It's all in the past.

That's a lie. Time does not heal all wounds. Many wounds become worse over time.)

What's Past has Not Passed

I (Melanie) was molested until I was about 13 years old. As I grew older, I really thought that I had put it behind me. I had tried to get on with my life but, as an adult and as a pastor's wife, no less, I found myself feeling hatred and contempt towards my grandfather. No, time does not heal all wounds. (The only thing that heals wounds is Jesus.)

I truly believed that time would cure the problem. As I became an adult, I continued to pray that enough time would pass for me to finally get over it. For years I prayed that I wouldn't be angry and hurt anymore.

I learned the hard way that it would not happen like that. One day, I happened to call my grandmother's house when I thought that she had returned home from a stay in the hospital. Unfortunately, she wasn't back yet, but my grandfather was there. He answered the phone, and said to me, "If you will come, we can have a really good time."

I immediately hung up the phone, and just sobbed and sobbed. I thought, "What would make him think that talking to me this way was okay?!?" How could he think that I, an adult woman, would find this appealing in any way? I felt violated all over again.

I became more and more angry. Anger snowballs. Oh, no–Time does not heal all wounds. You can bury it for a while, but it's always going to surface.

I (Steve) discovered that to also be true in my own life and I've seen it in the lives of others. While my injuries were trivial compared to the trauma of Melanie's experience, they were not unimportant. And neither are your hurts, even if you did not have traumatic offenses committed against you. Regardless of their size or origin, the painful events in our lives have a cumulative effect on us. They do affect us.

Harboring Unforgiveness Brews Tension

As a pastor, I had to tolerate the abuse of different people during my nearly 21 years in service. As I mentioned, I had no outlet for handling these offenses, no opportunity to vent my feelings about those kinds of things. So they began to have a cumulative effect on me. I think of it this way:

Imagine a coffee cup that is filled to the brim with scalding coffee. That was my emotions inside of me. Now, imagine me going out, getting in my car, and driving down a bumpy dirt road every day. That road was my lifestyle. The bumps in the road might have been an encounter with a critical church member, or might have been car trouble that suddenly happened. Maybe it was my young children playing too loudly downstairs, or any number of other insignificant issues that arise daily in everybody's life. It wasn't the size of the bump that was the problem for me. It was the fullness of the cup.

When we harbor unforgiveness, it affects us at an emotional level. Our emotional scale is set higher than that of a person who doesn't harbor unforgiveness. When your cup is that full of scalding coffee, you have to exercise great control for your own good, and for the good of those around you, because you really don't want to burn anybody. So you work hard at holding on to your cup without spilling its contents.

But no matter how hard you try, it just doesn't seem possible because, after all, the road is bumpy. So this quickly becomes a very tense way to live. In fact, sometimes it was enough to make a preacher cuss!

Understanding the True Meaning of Forgiveness

What do we do about this matter of forgiveness? After we acknowledge the gnawing ache of unforgiveness, the second step towards finding freedom over the things that have hurt you and the people who have offended you in life is to understand the true meaning of forgiveness.

First, let us establish a working definition for the word, "forgiveness." We encourage you to memorize this definition. It will be a good foundation for moving toward your own healing.

The definition of forgiveness is ("the deliberate choice to release a person from all obligations that he or she has toward me as a result of any offense that he or she has committed against me.")

Forgiveness is a choice: the choice to release somebody. (The key is *choosing to release the offender by discharging the debt you are owed.*) Never is the purity of grace seen more clearly than when we forgive.

It is possible to take another approach. It is possible to go back and look at the things that have happened to us and then try to analyze them. We can obsess on trying to figure out why things happened, exactly what was going on and understanding where God was when this took place. We can agonize over why He allowed this. It's a great expenditure of wasted energy. Melanie's story makes clear the reality about evil things in this world.

She says, "Things happen because we live in an evil world where evil things happen. There's nothing that you can do to control it."

There's nothing that you can do to control it. That's exactly right. (But there is a way that you can respond to what happens to you in this life that will prevent you from becoming enslaved and imprisoned by it.)

The Promise of Freedom: We Want to Forgive

Maybe you've been hurt in your past, and you feel that you are now forever connected to that offense, that you are forever connected to that person. If you don't forgive the one who has hurt you, you'll never be free from the person, and you'll never be free from that event.

The reason to examine and practice the way to forgive is so that we find freedom. That is the key word here–Freedom.

Nelson Mandela said about the moment he walked out of his prison on Robin Island, "As I walked out the door toward the gate that would lead to my freedom I knew if I didn't leave my bitterness and hatred behind I'd still be in prison."

In order to really appropriate freedom, we must understand the true meaning of forgiveness. That is, the deliberate and conscious choice to release a person from all obligation that they have towards us as a result of any offense that they've committed against us.

You might think, "Why would I want to forgive? The wrong done to me is unforgivable!" Those kinds of feelings are often normal and to be expected, but remember, this isn't about the person that hurt you. This is about *you* and your wholeness.

When we see our true selves, beneath the emotion, confusion and anger, we will actually discover that we want to forgive. We want to do what we need to do in order to be well and put the whole matter behind us.

We want to forgive because, at the core of our being, it is our nature to forgive. We have Jesus Christ living inside of us. In fact, He defines who we truly are, and *He is a Forgiver.*

We Have Been Forgiven

The greatest motivation for forgiving others is that we forgive because we have been forgiven. That's it– plain and simple. (You can forgive because you have been given forgiveness.)

I discuss this matter in depth in my book, **Unlock Your Bible**, when I explained how, when Jesus talked about forgiveness in the New Testament, He was speaking about the application of forgiveness during the age in which he lived, which was still under the

Covenant of Law. We don't live in that day or under that Covenant, today. We live in the day of Grace, and this makes a big difference when compared to what Jesus said to those who were still under the Law.

Because (the dividing line between all of history is the death, burial, and resurrection of Jesus Christ,) His teachings in Scripture fit perfectly within the context of the Law at the time He spoke them. When asked about the subject of forgiveness, Jesus often answered in what we might call the "rules of the day."

For example, in Matthew, chapter 6, when Jesus' disciples ask Him about how to pray, as far as forgiveness is concerned, He provides a model that we have come to know as the Lord's Prayer: "Forgive us our debts, as we forgive our debtors (those who trespass against us)."

He said, (forgive us as we forgive others.) He elaborates further on this issue of forgiveness under the Law system in Matthew 6:14-15: "If you forgive men for their transgressions, your Heavenly Father will also forgive you. But if you do not forgive men, then your Father will not forgive you your transgressions."

That was the Law in action: if you wanted God to do something for you, then you first had to do something to cause Him to act on your behalf.

Every time Jesus was asked for answers about forgiveness, He answered according to the Law. Fortunately, as you know, we now live under the New Covenant. Were we still living under the Law, and if there was any unforgiveness in your heart towards someone else, Jesus' words in Matthew 6:14-15 would apply. Basically, "If you don't forgive men, then your Father's not going to forgive you."

You *cannot apply verses written under the Old Covenant to you personally*. This is even true when it comes to the words that Jesus spoke to His Old Covenant audience.

If we could jump back to living under the Law, we could never be forgiven, ourselves. Certainly there have been times in our own lives, perhaps even now, where there's unforgiveness in our hearts towards someone else. Jesus plainly said, "If you do not forgive men, then your Father will not forgive you your transgressions." Thank God, that day has passed. The Old Covenant is gone, and a New Covenant now rules.

Do not believe it when someone cites these words, and says, "You better forgive others, or God won't forgive you."

It is not true.

You are already forgiven.

Your sins have been forgiven–past, present, and future, they have all been absolved by His finished work on the cross.

Emphasizing full forgiveness. Wants to promote confidence in full forgiveness in Christ. But going off rails.

Jesus Acted in Grace

While what Jesus taught was the Law in action, he always *acted* in grace throughout his personal relationships with other people. He couldn't help himself. He so loves us. He is so filled with grace!

There's an example in John 8 about a woman who was called an adulteress. When the Scribes and Pharisees pointed out that Moses commanded that adulterers be stoned, Jesus didn't dispute the Law. He just suggested that their application of the Law include themselves.

After His challenge that "the sinless one among them cast the first stone," the crowd dispersed until no one was left except for the woman who had been caught. Having acknowledged the validity of the Law, Jesus went on to demonstrate gracious forgiveness toward her.

He said to the woman, "Where are your accusers? Did nobody condemn you?"

And she said, "Not one, Lord."

Jesus said, "Neither do I condemn you. Go your way. From now on, sin no more."

That incident is so typical of Jesus during his earthly ministry. (He utilized the Law to raise awareness of sin, and then He demonstrated grace by His own behavior.)

You and I don't have the ability within ourselves to forgive all of those who have hurt us. But we can understand the true meaning of forgiveness by looking at Jesus, who released us from all obligations that we have toward Him as a result of the offenses we have committed against Him. Then we can forgive.

Please Recognize His Forgiveness

Do you know why we're able to do that? We're able to do it because we have been forgiven. That's exactly why. Before the cross, you see the teachings that say we forgive in order to get forgiveness. After the cross, we find in the Bible that we forgive because we have been forgiven.

For instance, here is a passage from Colossians 13:12-13:

> Therefore as the elect of God, holy and beloved, put on tender mercies, kindness, humility, meekness, long suffering, bearing with one another, and forgiving one another, if anyone has a complaint against another; (even as Christ forgave you, so you also must do.) (NKJV)

Another example of forgiveness under grace can be found in Ephesians 4:32: "Be kind to one another, tenderhearted, forgiving one another, (even as God in Christ forgave you.")

We forgive because we have been forgiven. That is the essence of forgiveness. Do you recognize that God has forgiven all your sins? You can't give what you don't know that you have.

All of your sins have been totally forgiven. Please be persuaded by that fact. Every sin that you have ever committed or ever will commit has been totally forgiven. Jesus took your sins, and He bore them upon Himself at the cross. He took your sins on Himself.

Colossians 2:13-14, (NKJV) says:

> And you, being dead in your trespasses and the uncircumcision of your flesh, He has made alive together with Him, having forgiven you all trespasses, having wiped out the handwriting of requirements that was against us, which was contrary to us. And He has taken it out of the way, having nailed it to the cross.

Here he talks about the certificates of death, or the handwriting of ordinances that was "against us," as some translations say. It's like an IOU, like an invoice that delineated all of the sins that you would commit in your whole lifetime, and Jesus took those sins upon himself. Then, when He had fully paid the debt that sin incurred for you, He said, "It is finished."

Your Debts are Paid in Full ...
So God Guides Us to Forgive

One word in the Greek language means, "It is finished." It's the word, *tetelestai.* Another way to translate that word is, "It is paid in full." Sin has been fully dealt with. Sin is a moot point now, because our sin has been dealt with by the finished work of Jesus Christ.

You will never experience the penalty for sin because your sin has been dealt with fully. You have been totally set free from it. Sin is now off the table. It is no longer an issue, thanks to Jesus.

People who have a hard time accepting total forgiveness for themselves have a hard time forgiving other people. But you have been forgiven. God is for you, and He has forgiven you of everything that you have ever done, or everything that you could or will do. It's because of that that we have the ability to forgive other people.

How would a person like Melanie forgive someone who did what her grandfather did to her, if it had not been for the forgiveness that she herself received in Jesus Christ? She knew that God was on her side, even in the midst of the horror that happened to her. He guided her, faithfully, through her circumstances, and demonstrated His love even at the darkest moments of her life.

What I (Melanie) know now is that God has always been with me. From the time that I was a small child, I've always felt the presence of the Lord in my life. I didn't grow up in a Christian family, but somehow I always knew that God was near to me, and that He was caring for me, even in the midst of any bad things going on. He wasn't *in what* was happening; but He was *in it with me* when that was happening.

He was on my side. I can look back now and say that God has used what happened to me because He is bigger than any wrong that happens to us. (He didn't, and wouldn't have, caused it to happen, but He redeemed my injury and pain, and has worked through it to accomplish good for others and glory for Him.)

Because we live in this kind of world, these kinds of things do happen. But the fact that I'm here and willing to openly discuss it right now, to help people who are hurting, says that He used it for good.

Satan meant it for evil. But God has used it for great good in my life, by giving me the opportunities to speak to other women. I have been able to offer them the freedom that can be theirs.

I'm not suggesting that what happened to me was a good thing, nor that I wanted it to happen. But it did. And God has used it to bring healing to other people's lives. I'm thankful for that.

God Wants Us to be Whole & Free

Your Heavenly Father has been in charge of your life every day that you've been on this planet. You may wonder why God would have allowed certain things to happen in your life. We cannot answer that question.

We do know that we serve a sovereign God who loves us, and that He superintends our lives from the day we're born all the way into eternity beyond this life. We simply have to entrust ourselves to Him.

Your Father loves you so much that He has totally forgiven you. He's forgiven you of every sin that you ever have committed. Every deed, every thought, and every word—He has forgiven you. It will never be held against you.

It is from that place that we can forgive other people. We don't forgive them for their sake. We forgive them for our sake. (We forgive because we have been forgiven. We forgive because it is our nature to forgive, because we have the divine nature of Jesus Christ living inside of us. We forgive because we want to be whole. We want to be well. We want to be free.)

◆ ◆ ◆
◆ ◆ ◆

God has Led You
To This Place of Forgiveness

Are you tired of being tied to your past?

Are you tired of the undercurrent of bitterness and resentment?

Are you tired of a melancholic soul that cannot find the joy that Jesus offers because you've not let go of something in your past?

Think back to the day that Jesus died for you. Our Heavenly Father lives in the eternal now. You and I experience life sequentially, but He sees everything happening simultaneously. When Jesus hung on that cross, He was looking at you. As He hung there, He was looking at your sins, your actions, your thoughts, and your words. It was from that place of the cross that He said, "I forgive you."

"I forgive you. For the sins of your lifetime, you will not be held responsible. You are forgiven. You're justified, as though you had never sinned in your life."

That's the gift that He's given to us.

(And because of that, we're now able to offer that gift to other people.)

You can spend the rest of your life trying to understand why things have happened in your life—or you can trust the Holy Spirit's voice as He speaks to you, and as He encourages you to release your unforgiveness and express forgiveness towards that one or those people who have brought you the hurt and the pain that you feel.

It's up to you. It may seem that the wrong done to you is unforgivable, but by His grace *you can do it.* I know, because I did. It wasn't by sheer willpower on my part either. It was a conscious choice that was empowered by the grace of God within me.

God has led you to this moment for a purpose. He's brought you right up to this very moment of reading the teaching in this book. Every day of your life, He has led you, step by step, and now He has brought you to the place where He's offering you freedom.

He's saying to you, "My child, I love you so much. I forgave you, and you walk in constant forgiveness with me. Now I give you the gift of forgiving others, so you don't have to walk in bondage, carrying that weight for the rest of your life.")

Will you do it? You *can* forgive what you have designated unforgivable. Not because you feel it. Not because what was done wasn't seriously wrong. (You can forgive because God has empowered you to forgive, and because you want to be done with it.)

Trust God and Glorify Him

In the next chapter, we will look at *how to forgive*, the actual mechanics of it. We will share how to apply the scriptural method in a very practical way, and give you detailed instruction on how to express forgiveness from your heart towards other people.

We understand this sovereign God who loves you from personal experience. We know how He can take the thing that has happened in your life, no matter what it might be, and turn it around so that you can honor Him through it with the healing that He gives to you.

The important thing to remember is that we serve a sovereign God who is over everything, good and bad.

When you know that God is sovereign, that He loves you, that He cares for you and wants what's best for you, you can look at your life and say, "That was a horrible thing that happened, but God is going to do something with my life, and in my life, because of it. I'm just going to trust Him to accomplish what He wants to, in and through me, so that my life will glorify Him."

(That's what we want in our lives–for God to be glorified in all things. If He can use the painful events in our lives to bring glory to Himself, then we'll just walk that path.)

He has written the days of our lives. Sometimes I (Melanie) have said to Steve that I don't like the story! "This part of the story is not good, and I wish that God would write it differently!" But He didn't. He wrote it *this* way.

He certainly didn't do evil, but He allowed evil to rear its ugly head, and He did for a reason. (So I'm going to live out the story that God has for me, and pray that it can bring glory to Him, that I can be of service to other people in helping to deliver them from the pain that they suffer.)

The true meaning of forgiveness is to release people from all obligations that they have towards us, as the result of any offense they have committed against us.

We hope that you see God's hand in your life, and how He has led you to this place. We hope that you continue to move forward through these chapters, step by step, towards that point at which you will forgive and release the one who has hurt you.

♦ ♦ ♦
♦ ♦ ♦

3

What To Do

Melanie and I responded to the offenses and hurts in our lives by building up a protective barrier between the outside world and ourselves. We learned how to cope, and how to manage life so that we could minimize the possibility for future offenses. We learned how to live in such a way as to try and get our needs met.

(We all build these flesh patterns around the offenses that have happened in our lives.) And the only way to be free from the tyranny of the flesh, the only way to walk from our true identity in Christ concerning the matter of unforgiveness, is to release that unforgiveness, and to choose to forgive those who have hurt us.

We have been forgiven, and it is for that reason that we have the motivation to forgive others. The Bible says that God demonstrated His love toward us in that, while we were yet sinners, Christ died for us.

The greatest expression of forgiveness ever demonstrated in this world took place when Jesus died on the cross. We've done nothing to deserve that forgiveness. Still, God chose to love us, and to provide a way for us to be forgiven totally.

So, the pattern was established at the cross. Before the cross, people forgave in order to get forgiveness. Since the cross, we forgive because we have been forgiven.

And forgiveness is a choice.

We want to share specifically how to forgive other people.

Misunderstanding Small Hurts May Prevent our Gaining Freedom

There are some errors that keep us in bondage.

While Melanie's offense was traumatic, the offenses against me (Steve), a pastor, may seem trivial to you, and I've sometimes felt hesitant even to mention them in much detail. But I share my story, as well, because it's important for you to know that you don't have to have had some type of life-altering event in your life in order to create the need forgive other people.

When the Holy Spirit began to bring memories of hurts back into my mind, I thought of the many offenses that I had received, over the years. There were people who had hurled insults and injury at me. Many of those were petty. For example, early on in my ministry, there were people who were critical because the lights were left on in our house too late at night. They wondered how late we were staying up because, in that place, the church paid our utility bill for us. So some nitpicking people wondered why we burned the lights at all times of the day and night.

I've had long-time members of churches who had gained leadership positions make it their goal to dissect everything that they could find in order to criticize me. They sought to turn others against me. Sometimes, they lied. They postured. They manipulated. Then, they would act in leadership meetings as if they were as pure as the driven snow.

Those are the kinds of things that gnaw at you, as a pastor. While they usually aren't major events, the constant harassment of critics can wear a man down.

Once, Melanie went to church wearing a new dress that her mother had given her for her birthday. At this church, our salary had been cut three times. Somebody at the church actually had the nerve to say, "Well, you must be getting decent enough pay. She's wearing brand new clothes."

Pastors don't really have a comeback for that kind of remark. But, over the years, there were multiple times where people would say such insensitive things. Sometimes, they couldn't be easily dismissed as not being critical. In fact, at times they were blatant attacks.

There was one person who tried to ruin me. She even went so far as to contact churches where I had served, prior to her own church, and try to dig up anything that she could in order to try to hurt and discredit me where I served as pastor.

As God began to work into me the awareness that I needed to forgive, those kinds of things came bubbling up from beneath the surface of my consciousness. (Remember, the life of Christ is that river of living water that wants to flow from us like an artesian well, but unforgiveness becomes a barrier that keeps us from being able to experience that outflow of His life.) When the Lord began to work in me, those things began to churn up, and I discovered that there were many, many things like that that I needed to forgive.

I recognize that they may be perceived as trivial compared with Melanie's legitimately traumatic experience of being sexually molested. But these experiences had (impacted and affected me, nonetheless.)

Maybe the offenses against you have seemed small or trivial. Maybe they've been traumatic and huge.

It doesn't matter.

If you haven't addressed the offenses against you properly, and dealt with them through forgiveness, they will have an accumulative effect on you. They interfere with your spiritual walk, and keep you from living the life you were made to live.

→ (*Forgiveness: They Don't Deserve It, And You Pay the Price*)

Forgiving people is not an easy thing to do, but it is possible because of the Christ who lives in us. We need to choose to do it, and then apply the scriptural method for forgiveness. Part of why it is difficult is this that there is a cost to the person who forgives.

David Augsberger wrote a great book on forgiveness called "The New Freedom of Forgiveness."[4] He writes:

(A man who forgives pays a tremendous price: the price of the evil he forgives) If the state pardons a criminal, society bears the burden of the criminal's deed. If I break a priceless heirloom that you treasure, and you forgive me, you bear the loss and I go free. Suppose I ruin your reputation? To forgive me,

---

[4] David Augsberger, *The New Freedom of Forgiveness*, Moody Publishers, 2000.

you must freely accept the consequence of my sin, and let me go free. (In forgiveness, you bear your own anger and wrath at the sin of another voluntarily accepting responsibility for the hurt he has inflicted on you.)

Then he adds:

"To forgive is costly. To forgive is to carry one's own wrath for the sin of another. The guilty one is released. (The offended one frees him by bearing his own indignation, and resolving it in love. God forgives by carrying his own wrath on the sin that we've embraced expressed against Him. He absorbs our guilt, and makes us free. Forgiveness goes through the sin to freedom."

So you say, "Wow! I'm the one who has to pay the price?"

That's right.

We will state it plainly and simply: the person who you need to forgive doesn't deserve it.

If they deserved it, it wouldn't be forgiveness, because forgiveness is an expression of grace towards someone else. Grace is unmerited.

So, no, they don't deserve it!

But you don't forgive people because they deserve it. You forgive people because you need to do it. You forgive not for them, but for yourself. — secondary

There's a passage in Isaiah 43:25, where our God says: "I'm the one who blocks out your transgressions or your sins for my own sake."

Bad hermeneutics He blots out your sins and forgives you for *His* sake.

In the same way, we forgive others for *our* own sakes because, if we don't forgive, then those offenses against us fester within us, and their poisonous effects taint our whole life. We may be aware of the effect or we may have no idea of what lies dormant deep in our emotions.

As an example of this, Melanie describes in more detail the day when her mother called her about her grandfather's deteriorating health. The Lord told her this very same thing: that she could be free from the terrible offense that had been committed against her.

How the Lord Guided Melanie to Freedom

My (Melanie) mother called and told me that my grandfather was in the hospital, and that he might not live. I know that she was asking me to pray for him. She expected that. We never talked about it, so I don't know what she really heard, but I was so angry. It had to be clear to her. There was no way that I was going to pray for this man.

I was filled with anger and even rage, and told her, "Good! He's finally going to die. I actually thought that, one day, we would walk in and find that he had nasty-ed away. I had long imagined that we would just find a pile of ashes on the floor, because that's what his end would be." Then I told her, "I'm so glad that he's finally going to die and go to hell."

I know that my mother didn't know what to do with that. There I was, a grown woman with four children, a pastor's wife, and she was expecting compassion from me. But that's not what she got! She got all of my anger.

My mother just didn't understand it. But for my part, it *scared* me, because I didn't know that I had that kind of hatred inside of me. I didn't know that I had those kinds of feelings. I really did want him to die and go to hell. I wasn't just saying that. I really did feel that way, and I wouldn't have care if he had.

But as soon as I hung up the phone, the presence of God became real to me in such a powerful way. There's no denying it. There's no saying that it was anything other than that. I was overwhelmed by the awareness of His presence.

I just told Him, "God, I don't know what to do with these feelings. I didn't know that I felt this kind of hatred. How could I come to this place in my life, where I would hate anything or anybody this much?" I just didn't know it was possible for someone who truly loved the Lord to have these kinds of feelings. I asked him, "What can I do?"

I didn't really expect the answer that I got.

The Lord told me, "You need to forgive him."

That wasn't the answer I would have expected Him to give me.

I said, "Forgive him! How could I possibly forgive him? This man does *not* deserve forgiveness. He doesn't deserve to go to heaven. He deserves only hell, so why should I forgive him?"

And then I heard the Lord speak to me again. He said, "Melanie, what have *you* done to deserve Heaven?"

That was hard. It was very hard to hear.

I answered, "Nothing, Lord. I didn't do anything to deserve heaven. So, what do I do?"

Again, He told me very plainly, "You must forgive him."

So that's what I did. I actually began to speak out loud. I'd never done that before. No one had ever told me to do anything like this, but I just felt compelled to speak the words aloud.

(I called him by name and I said, "I forgive you for every evil thing that you've ever done to me. I release you from any debt that I feel you have ever owed me.")

Then I went a step further, but only because I was

compelled by the Lord to do it. I added, "I will never bring this up again. It's over, and you're forgiven."

I can't describe the feeling that came over me then–the lightness and the joy that filled my soul, things that had been absent for so long. I didn't realize what a heavy weight I had been carrying around.(I had been carrying this unforgiveness all my life.

At that moment, I was released. The Lord gave me the power to do it–because He did empower me to do it. I couldn't have done it on my own. He empowered me to forgive. I released my grandfather, and never took it back.)

The Power & Process of Release

It's important to know that when we forgive we don't always feel that kind of immediate relief, but I did on that occasion. (The evidence of having forgiven isn't an immediate change of feelings. That may take time. But the act of forgiveness is real, however long it takes.)

Melanie released her grandfather. She did this without anyone having taught her about how to forgive. The Holy Spirit showed her what to do, and demonstrated that to forgive is to *release* a person from all obligations that they have towards us as a result of any offense they have committed against us.

Read the prayer below and see if you can agree with it in your heart:

Father, would you show the people reading this book the hurts that they have experienced and those people whom they need to forgive? Would you bring that to the mind of the one who reads this paragraph right now?

Does anything pop into your mind? Does anybody come into your thoughts?

When I (Steve) walked through this matter of forgiving those who had hurt me, it was a process. I spent several weeks identifying those who had hurt me, and writing down their names. I went through the steps of identifying the type of offense that they had committed against me, and I followed a process that I'm now going to describe to you.

I ask that you do this homework, as well. These steps comprise what some have called, "The Forgiveness Exercise."

❦ *The Forgiveness Exercise*

This exercise is not original with us, so maybe you've heard about it before, or even read this in somebody's book. You may know a counselor who has done this process. I (Steve) have had people take offense at these teachings, saying, "Oh, I've known psychiatrists and psychologists who have done that."

That doesn't bother me. I've known of psychologists and psychiatrists who have used electricity and watched TV, eaten at the table, and done a lot of other things that I do. Truth is truth. But what I'm about to challenge you to do is not a psychological or psychiatric approach to anything. It is a biblical focus. The framework may be similar to something that you have heard from others, but the following is a biblical approach to forgiveness.

This is the practical application of the scriptural method for forgiveness.

1. Take a pad or piece of paper, and begin to pray that the Holy Spirit will show you the memories or mental images of the people who have hurt you. Ask Him to reveal them to you.

Some names may come flooding into your mind as soon as you read this, but don't be move forward with this exercise prematurely. If, instead, you wait on the Lord, He may bring names and people to your mind that you haven't even thought about.

I like the psalmist's prayer, "Search me, oh Lord. You search me, oh God, and see if there be any unclean way in me."

Unforgiveness is that unclean obstacle down in our soul that keeps the river of living water from flowing forth. So pray, and ask the Lord to show you who might have hurt you.

When He does, write each name down on your piece of paper. It's important that you write down the names of the people. Sometimes, there's underlying anger or an underlying sense of unforgiveness, but we haven't specifically pinpointed which people have hurt us, nor the specifics of those events. It's important to do that. So write down the names.

2. Write down exactly what they did to you. Be specific. You might be tempted to say, "Well, they always did this" or "they were always doing that." Okay, so think of a certain thing or a specific instance when they did that thing, and write it down. Let this example represent all of the other times. Write down exactly what they did to you, on that occasion, and be specific.

I can't stress that enough: *be specific*.

3. Write down how that made you feel, when it happened. At this point you may think, "Steve, why would you have me dredge up all that stuff?"

I remember when the counselor who led me forward in the training that I did told me to do this step, I said, "You know what? Man, some of that stuff has been buried for a long time. It smelled bad when I buried it, and I can't imagine, if we go digging it up, how it's going to smell now after all this time!"

But it is important to take this third step.

Write down how you felt at the time.

Why do I tell you to do that? (Because you need to have the Holy Spirit re-attach the emotional significance of the event to the event, itself.) Some of us have suppressed feelings, and when we look back, even if we remember the event, the memory is cold, callous, and sterile.

(Before you can fully forgive somebody, you have to understand the cost. You have to know the weight of the offense against you.)

For instance, let's suppose you were in a store and I came in and said, "Listen, I need to tell you something. I just backed into your car in the parking lot. I hit your car when I was trying to pull into a parking space. Will you forgive me?"

What would you say?

You'd say, "You hit my car?!"

"Yeah, would you forgive me?"

I know what you'd be thinking. First, how much damage did it do? Did it scuff the bumper? Did it smash the rear quarter panel? You'd want to know the amount of damage done before you'd extend forgiveness, if you would extend it at all.

(The same is true of the offenses against us. You need to identify the amount, the weight, the cost of the offense against you, so that you can then forgive and release the person)

Don't just rush through this. Don't just write down a name and say, "Yeah, but I forgive 'em."

I have counseled certain people who weren't yet ready to forgive, because they hadn't taken ownership of the offense against them. You have to own the hurt. And this may be a painful thing, allowing the Holy Spirit to re-attach the weight of a given event to your memory of it. But it's important for you to allow Him to do that.

I'm not talking about trying to work up emotion or anything like that. I'm just saying that(you need to be honest about how you felt.)

When you're writing down how you felt at that time, you might (also write down what that communicated to you about yourself.) What life message did you get from that? What did that speak to you about you, as a person?

Some of us live with a faulty self-image. We have developed a false image of who we are because somebody, somewhere, back down the road,(put a label on us through an offense that they committed against us, and we owned it.)

At this point in your exercise, you also need to identify the message that each offense communicated to you about yourself.

4. Then, you need to forgive the person. There is more than one way to do this. What we offer here is not a law or some legalistic formula. It is a process that we have found helpful, however, as have multitudes of other people who have put this Forgiveness Exercise into practice.

Take a chair and sit it in front of you in an empty room. Sit down in front of that chair by yourself, and imagine that one specific person on your list is in that chair.

Then, begin to speak to that person. Call them by name, as though they were sitting right there. Next, recount out loud exactly what they did to you, and how it made you feel.

Do you think that you might feel foolish, talking into thin air? Maybe you will, but I promise that you'll get over it, once you start.

Reading about this step, you may say, "That sounds silly."

Okay. If it sounds too silly, and you don't want to do it, you don't have to do it. This is not a law. It is not some magic formula, not some legalistic prescription that must be done this way, and only this way.

However, this is the well that I drank from, and I found my thirst quenched. Melanie did, too. So did many other people whom I've counseled, and countless others who have been counseled in this technique by others.

It works if the Holy Spirit is in it.

Imagine that they're in that chair. Talk to them about what they did, and how it made you feel. And then, you forgive them.

How do you forgive? You release them.

That's what Melanie said: "I released my grandfather."

You might say something like this out loud: ("I forgive you for what you did to me, and I release you from anything and everything that you might owe me for that. From this day forward, you don't owe me anything for what you have done. You are forgiven, because I forgive you.")

Don't say, "I want to forgive you."

If you want to, just do it.

Don't say, "I'd like to forgive you."

If you'd like to, just do it!

Say the words: "I forgive you for what you did." When you have expressed that forgiveness from your heart, that nails down the moment that you forgave. It's not the words: it's the attitude of your heart. It's the *conscious choice* that you have made to release that person, and to forgive them.

There's freedom in that, because forgiveness <u>is</u> a choice.

I will admit to you that this exercise is not easy. You may start the exercise, for example, and then when you begin to write down names–particularly when you begin to write down what they did and how it made you feel–you may hear the enemy whisper this in your mind: "This is silly. This is ridiculous. I'm not doing this!"

But I caution you: please don't short-circuit this process. The Holy Spirit will be working in this. If you stop prematurely, you may rob yourself of what God wants to do, through you and in you, in this situation.

See This Exercise Through

We really want to reiterate this word of caution. Don't stop this exercise midway through it. It is so tragic. We have seen so many people begin this important process of identifying their hurts and the people who have hurt them. They start to make this list, and, in their memory, reliving the moments and dredging up the painful past because they know that it needs to be done. But then, they stop short of the process of forgiveness.

How horrible, because it only makes things worse in their lives. If they don't go on to forgive, what they have done is to pull up all of this pain from their past, and then talk about it, so their emotions have intensified. But without completing the exercise, they feel worse than they did at the beginning.

Don't stop the process. If you want freedom, please do what we're recommending that you do. Start *Summary:* these steps. (Ask the Holy Spirit to show you the names, write them down, identify your hurts, and follow through. Release the people. Go ahead and forgive them.

You need to mentally place each person on your list in a chair, and then talk out loud to them. Tell them exactly how you feel about what they did to you.

Then, verbally express to that person, "I forgive you. And I release you from any debt you owe me."

We can't express enough to you how important this is going to be in your healing process.)

✦ *A Scriptural Method With a Biblical Theme*

Melanie demonstrated the scriptural method for forgiveness in the way that she expressed forgiveness towards her grandfather.

We haven't used an abundance of Bible verses in this teaching, up to this point. If you've studied other topics with me (Steve), you know that I teach a lot from the Bible, often verse by verse. But nevertheless, these are biblical teachings. The theme here is a biblical theme, and the essence of what we are saying is grounded in the Scripture. This part of the teaching, this description of how to express forgiveness, is a specifically scriptural method.

You might wonder, "How can what you've said, about identifying the people who hurt you, then exactly what they did, and how it caused you to feel, making specific notes of the debt they had to you, and, finally, choosing to forgive them, expressing that forgiveness—in what way is that biblical?"

Let's look at the death of Jesus. Everything comes from out of the cross. We can't completely offer forgiveness towards others until we have believed the truth about the complete forgiveness that we ourselves have received from Jesus Christ. (We are motivated to forgive because Jesus has forgiven us.)

You can't work this up, yourself. So don't take these steps towards forgiveness and try to turn them into some formula, because, if you do, you'll end up with just another dead, legalistic approach to your problem.

But if you appropriate the reality of the indwelling life of Christ, and say, ("Lord Jesus, you're my life, and you've forgiven me. Now, by your life, by your grace, by your power, I'm going to forgive those who have hurt me,") that's an altogether different matter. This method is neutral in and of itself. But if these steps are impregnated with Divine Life, it's altogether different. It does become a scriptural method for forgiveness.

How is this scriptural?

First of all, when you forgive somebody, it's *substitutionary*. By that I mean, (you bear the price for what they did, just like Jesus bore the consequence for our sin.) In the same way, when we forgive other people, we bear the price for what they have done. So, it's substitutionary.

Second, it's *underserved*. I've mentioned that some readers will say, "They don't deserve to be forgiven." So let me reiterate: it wouldn't be forgiveness if they deserved it. Forgiveness is totally undeserved. It is an act of grace. Ephesians 2: 8-9 says, "For by grace you have been saved through faith, and that not of yourselves; it is the gift of God, not of works, lest anyone should boast."

We don't deserve it. It's undeserved, this forgiveness that Christ has extended to us. It's undeserved.

So, when you forgive somebody, you're doing a God-thing. It's scripturally sound, when you forgive.

Third, it is biblical because it is *unilateral*. I love the verse in Romans 5:8 that says, "While we were still sinners, Christ died for us."

Sometimes people ask, "Do you have to go to the person whom you forgive, and talk to them?" No, you don't have to do that.

Should you? Well, it depends. You have to pray about that, because there's no pat answer for that question.

In my (Melanie) case, I did not go to my grandfather, because I didn't feel led by the Holy Spirit to do that. I felt that it would create more problems, and stir up a greater mess than it would solve. So I simply forgave him. What you do is up to you, guided by what the Holy Spirit shows you.

In either case, we want you to see that the choice to forgive somebody is unilateral. (They don't even have to ask to be forgiven. "While we were yet sinners, Christ died for us." So He forgave us before we even asked.)

The Apostle Paul wrote, "God was in Christ, reconciling the world to himself, *no longer counting people's sins against them"* (2 Corinthians 5:19, NLT; emphasis added). That happened two thousand years ago, before any of us asked to be forgiven. It was a unilateral act of grace.

In the same way, we forgive others, whether they ask or not. It's a unilateral act on our part. They don't have to do anything for us to forgive them.

We hope that you'll pray about how to apply this scriptural method in your own life, and really practice these steps. Don't just let this go into your head. Please carry out the exercise that we've described in this chapter.

The next will address how to continue to walk in forgiveness towards those who have hurt us. What do you do if that person is still alive? Or, more specifically, what do you do if they continue their offenses towards you? How do you deal with that?

Let the Holy Spirit work this practice deeply within you until it becomes a part of your spiritual DNA.

4

Walking It Out Each Day

Forgiveness is the deliberate choice to release that person from all obligations they have towards us as a result of any offense they've committed against us. Melanie's story demonstrates how the Holy Spirit, by God's grace, empowered her to forgive. Whatever your offenses in life might be, you can forgive, as well.

Some people reading these pages may have had offenses equal to or perhaps even greater than what Melanie experienced. Many others may be more like Steve, whose hurts arose from offenses by people in the church who had been insensitive, people who had been critical of him, of Melanie, or our children. He had to forgive them in the same way that Melanie forgave her grandfather.

Once again, we don't want you to underestimate the importance of forgiveness, even in the absence of some horrible traumatic event in your life.

I (Melanie) forgave my grandfather, with the miraculous assistance of the Lord, before I had received any teaching of forgiveness, or even knew who I was in Christ. I didn't know anything about going through any kind of forgiveness exercise. What I did was totally what the Holy Spirit showed me to do. I just walked in that, moment by moment, as the Holy Spirit revealed to me what I needed to do in order to forgive.

In this chapter, we are going to look at the ways to walk in it, after you have forgiven. In Melanie's instance, after she forgave her grandfather, he didn't die immediately. He lived for a number of years after that. So how did she move forward to walk in forgiveness in the coming days?

Walking in Forgiveness Around Those Who have Hurt Us and Aren't Sorry

Many people have a mistaken notion of what forgiveness is, so I (Steve) think that it is really interesting how Melanie describes what forgiveness looked like, in her life, given the fact that her grandfather was still in her family. She had to decide whether she felt a need to reach out and express forgiveness to him, one-on-one.

Everywhere I go, people ask me the same question: how should someone deal with this, because these offenders often may still in their lives. I'm sure it's different for different people because the dynamics in various situations are different from one another. How do you deal with this situation? Like me, you probably have people in your life who try to manage what's going on. They want to manage how you respond through it.

For me (Melanie), I knew that I had forgiven. I knew that I wanted to continue to walk in that newfound freedom. But it didn't mean that I wanted to go and be a part of my offender's life anymore. (My grandfather had given up the right to be a part of my life. He hadn't changed.)So, to me, there was no point in my going and trying to establish a relationship with someone who had forfeited that right. He was still someone who was not sorry, someone who would not admit any wrongdoing.

I did not go and try to establish some kind of a relationship that was not there. I had been the wounded child, so it was up to him to establish a relationship with me. But the kind of relationship that he formed was a terrible, wrong relationship. So he didn't have a right to be in my life. And I certainly wasn't going to take my children to be with him. It was a matter of me walking it out, while taking care of my children through this process as well.

It is important to state this(again: it is not necessary for a person to be sorry for what they've done for you to forgive them.)Don't let this slip past you.

Before you were ever born, before you ever committed your first sin, certainly before you ever had a chance to be sorry and repent of your sin, Jesus paid for your sin. He provided forgiveness at the cross.

In the same way, we don't have to wait until somebody is sorry for what she has done to us in order for us to forgive her. We can forgive even in the absence of her sorrow, or without her asking for forgiveness. Again, we forgive the person, not for their sake but for our sake.

But it does make a difference, once you forgive someone in the way that Melanie forgave her grandfather.

Taking Down the Walls

It made a huge difference. I (Melanie) had formed many walls in my life to protect myself from being hurt. So, the walls came down. I had this picture that the Lord gave me of (the cross coming down and tearing apart the walls of self-protection that I had built up in my life.)

Then I was able to allow people into my life. I was able to begin to trust people again. Until then, I had held people at arm's length because I didn't want to be hurt by anyone.

When you start to build walls, you hold the bad things out, but you also hold the good things out too. When you begin to let the walls come down, it happens a little at a time, almost like brick by brick. You can't do it all at one time. Your Father reveals to you the walls that you have built in your life in different areas. So, brick by brick, He began to take my walls down and I began to trust. I began to be able to see good in people whereas I was very skeptical of everyone until then.

Some of you have found yourselves in that same position. What Melanie says about building walls is very important. Again, as she said, when you build walls to protect yourself, you don't only shut out the bad things. You shut out the good.

Maybe you have seen evidence of unforgiveness in your own life by not being able to experience a sense of closeness or intimacy with people. Maybe you've been suspicious of friends. Maybe you've kept folks at arm's length because of walls that you've put up. You call yourself withdrawn and isolated, but in reality, it's a wall of unforgiveness that's been a barrier in your life.

As Melanie said, she built flesh patterns (coping mechanisms) around this incident, and those flesh patterns involved putting up walls that isolated and insulated herself from other people. We encourage you to let the Holy Spirit show you who you need to forgive, and then go ahead and do that.

Freed From Prison ...
But Anger Whispers Still

As Melanie walked in forgiveness after the moment she forgave her grandfather, she had to deal with the fact that the man was still alive, even though our family didn't see him often. She had a permanent change in her perspective, but that didn't mean that tinges of anger and resentment never arose again.

Instantly upon forgiving my grandfather, my feelings were changed. I knew that God had delivered me. When Steve came home from the church that day,

I told him about the miracle that had happened in my life. I told him that I had been divinely delivered. There was no other way to describe it. I knew that God had released me from all the pain that I had carried for so long.

So, it was instant. But, as time moved on, I began to have flashbacks that came to me out of nowhere. I would be tempted to feel angry again, to take on hurt again. When that happened, I would immediately just say "No!" I would remind myself: ("God delivered you from this. So why would you want to take it back?")

When those feelings came up, I would turn away from them. But it would happen again and again and again. When his name came up in our family, yes, I would be tempted to say bad things about him, and sometimes I still would, even though I knew better. But I would be reminded again. The Holy Spirit would gently speak to me and ask, "Do you really want to go back there?"

Once you've been delivered, once you've been freed from prison, you don't want to go back to prison!

That's the way that I felt–that I had lived for many, many years in a prison, and Jesus gave me the key. He caused me to walk out. So, no, I didn't want to walk back in.

I reminded myself, over and over again, of what God had done for me in freeing me. And that's what gave me forward movement. I found the motivation not to turn back, through that realization.

Feelings may still come back to you when you have forgiven somebody. But when you experience them, acknowledge that feelings are not the measurement of truth regarding what you've done in terms of forgiveness.

Practical Steps for Living with Forgiveness

Let us offer you some practical things that we hope will help you to walk in the forgiveness that you extend to other people.

First, when you have forgiven–when you've applied the scriptural method for forgiveness–*remind yourself* that you have, indeed, forgiven. Just because you have feelings that arise within you doesn't mean that you have not forgiven the person.

Forgiveness is the deliberate choice to release a person. So, it's a choice that you make at a given moment in time in your life. Once you have forgiven that person, it's a done deal. Feelings can come back and you may be tempted to think that you did not forgive the person. But, again, forgiveness is not tied to how you feel. Forgiveness revolves around whether or not you have chosen to forgive. If you did, then remind yourself of that.

(Second, in dealing with the person, continue to *maintain a zero balance* with them. Remember, that person now owes you nothing. You've forgiven the debt.)Sometimes, when people have hurt you, they'll keep on with the bad behavior.

In Melanie's case, she moved away when she reached adolescence, and certainly her grandfather never physically bothered her anymore after that. But there were times when he would be present while we were with family. As she said, this would stir up feelings in her again. Maybe he would say certain things, not even of a perverse nature, or he had certain mannerisms that triggered those feelings in her again. (She needed to keep that forgiveness account at a zero balance.)

With you, maybe it's somebody who keeps doing the same thing over and over again. What do you do? You say, "I've forgiven them, but they don't stop doing it."

The answer is exactly what Jesus said to Peter, when Peter asked, "How many times should we forgive? Seven?" And Jesus said, "No. Seventy times seven."

In other words, there is no limit to forgiveness. We are able to do that because we have been forgiven, and that's the only way that you can do it.

Ephesians, 4:32 says, "forgiving each other, just as Christ has also forgiven you." When you trusted in Christ, that wasn't the end of your sin, was it? You don't now behave sinlessly all the time, do you? You still lapse into sin, and yet your Heavenly Father maintains a zero balance with you. He keeps you, He

God :

(relates to you, in a posture of forgiveness because of the finished work of Christ.)

(In the same way, you need to relate to those who might continue to hurt you from a posture of forgiveness.)

You may have negative feelings. That's okay. Our third suggestion is this: acknowledge your feelings. (Surrender those feelings to God.)They're His problem, not yours.

You may sense anger rise up in you. Ephesians 4:26 says, "Be angry and do not sin." You can still feel anger arise in you. That's not something you have control over. It's how you address that feeling, however, that becomes the important issue.

There may be situations in which you might need to draw boundaries and forbid the person from continuing the bad behavior. In suggesting that forgiveness is vital, we aren't advocating that the right thing to do is allow the offender to keep doing what they're doing. Grace often empowers us to stand up and let it be known, in no uncertain terms, that the wrong action will stop and stop now. Every situation is different. The Holy Spirit will show you how to move ahead in your own circumstances.

However you proceed, deal with the negative feelings in a healthy way. Maintain the zero sum balance, and lay your feelings out before the Lord. You don't even have to ask Him to forgive you for what you're feeling because those feelings are spontaneous. They're an involuntary emotional reaction to what happened, and to the person whom you have to encounter. You just lay those feelings down before Him, and you acknowledge them. You don't have to feel guilty about them.

The key is to not act on your feelings, just to acknowledge them for what they are, and then move on. Once more for emphasis: "moving on" may mean confronting the wrongdoing, or it may mean putting it behind you. Divine guidance will make clear which to do.

Choose how you are going to behave based on who you are. That's how you deal with the feelings:

Feelings :

- ❖ You maintain a zero balance

- ❖ You affirm that you have forgiven

- ❖ Then, you set your heart towards the Lord, and relate to that person only in the way that the Holy Spirit leads you to relate to that person.

Led by the Holy Spirit

Walking in forgiveness is such a key to victory over painful experiences of the past. Don't let yourself be pulled back into the dark place from which you have been set free.

It's so important that we understand the reality of forgiveness in our lives, and that we (know that the ability to forgive is from God, Himself. We forgive because He has forgiven us.)

Through the truths we have shared in this book, you will be able to look at your own life and see God orchestrating, from start to finish, the details of your life that will bring you to the place of forgiveness.

There was nothing that I (Melanie) had ever read or anything that I had ever heard that caused me to react the way that I did, that day. I reacted to what the

Holy Spirit was teaching me. Alongside the teaching you've been given here, He will guide you too.

God came to me, and told me that I needed to forgive. That came out of nowhere, because it wasn't within me to forgive.

I've said before, I'd wished my grandfather dead and in hell so many times. But my Heavenly Father came to me and spoke to me. He let me see that I had hatred that was destroying me. It had caused me to build up walls. It had caused me to mistrust people. God showed me–and it only came from Him–that what I needed to do was to forgive. In releasing my grandfather from the evil things that he had done, I was really releasing myself. Then, and only then, could I walk in freedom.

I don't think that anybody could have shown me that, apart from Him speaking to me. He had to reveal it to me, to speak it to me in my spirit. Sometimes people can say the words, but it's the Holy Spirit that brings it to life, and brings it to light. That's what He did that day. That's what we pray is happening as you read this book.

Removing the Weight: A Future of Freedom

So many people say that they have forgiven someone, but they say, "I've forgiven, but I'm not going to forget."

It's true that you can't change the history. Neither will you get amnesia about the matter. You can't go back and rewrite what happened, but (you do have the power to change your future. You don't have to live in the past.) You have a new future that's waiting for you, and it's a future with freedom. One with the Holy Spirit working in your life, causing you to walk in freedom; a life that you never thought was possible. (You have the ability for your future to be a different one than it would be, if you continued to walk in unforgiveness.)

People who have been sexually abused sometimes come to Melanie–folks who have experienced similar abuse, and who really connect to her and her story. Others come forward who have had other kinds of traumatic hurts.

Because those who hurt me didn't leave as traumatic an imprint on me as Melanie's abuser had done, I (Steve) thought that it wasn't necessary for me to forgive. One time, I asked a friend, "Do you believe that I should officially forgive everybody who's hurt me? I don't see the need to forgive, because to forgive them would be to assign them greater importance in my life than I'm willing to admit they have."

I even went on to say, "You know, if I see a flea on me, I don't forgive. I just thump it away. If a flea bites me, I just flick it away with my finger. These folks are like irritating fleas to me. They don't have any real effect on me."

I look back at that now and see the hidden anger in that statement. Do you need to forgive incidental things, as well as major things? Yes!

Melanie forgave in an instant in the kitchen, by the work of the Holy Spirit. By contrast, my experience of forgiving past hurts was a little different.

I've described how I had been going through some training with my discipleship counselor. He had told me to sit and write down on paper the things that we described in chapter three. As I did that, God came to reveal my angry flesh patterns to me. He caused me to see the need to forgive people whom I had never thought that I'd needed to forgive, before. He basically started dismantling all of my defenses against forgiving until I was left with nothing but the decision as to whether or not I was going to be obedient to Him.

So, while with Melanie it happened in an instant, in my case, I wrestled with anger for several weeks. I pained about the offenses that I had written down on that piece of paper. I didn't want to forgive. But, on the other hand, more than I didn't want to forgive, I did want to forgive.

I felt the weight of the offenses that people had laid on me. I was very aware that they didn't deserve to be forgiven. And yet, because it's our nature to forgive, I wanted to. I wanted to be free from the past transgressions that had been committed towards me. I wanted to be free from the suppressed anger that had manifested itself as a tension inside of me for so many years.

I was reminded of Isaiah 43:25, where God said, "I'm the one who wipes out your transgressions for my own sake."

I wanted to forgive for my sake.

I wanted to forgive because I had been forgiven, and because I wanted to experience Him more intimately, without the barrier of unforgiveness keeping me from seeing His face clearly.

I was hurting, I was scared, but I did want to forgive, because it's our nature to do that. So that's what I did.

In my case, somebody else was with me. I sat in the office in the company of my discipleship counselor, and I talked to that empty chair where I imagined each person was sitting. I recounted each offense aloud, and expressed how I felt, how their offense had affected me. I shed tears as I did. I had suppressed a lot of emotion over these things, so tears streamed down my cheeks. But I chose to forgive.

I cancelled the debt, and acknowledged that the people who had hurt me owed me nothing. In fact, that night I took home the paper on which I had written all of those offenses, took it outside, and burned it. I'll never forget the smoke of that burning paper because, for some reason, it had an unusually offensive smell. But I watched that smoke disappear into the night sky, and I thanked God that it was going away, just like the offensive odor of unforgiveness was disappearing from my life.

I affirmed to God that I would walk in forgiveness toward people from that night forward. I thanked Him, because He'd given me the ability to forgive. In fact, I remember turning my face towards heaven, and whispering out loud, "Thank God I'm free at last."

Ask God for the Power to Let Hurt Go

We share our stories with you about forgiving and walking in forgiveness because it is a common challenge. It is the single most important way we know to get past the hurt when others have wrong you.

This matter of unforgiveness is very common. Melanie built walls, and the walls shut out the good as well as the bad. Unforgiveness created an underlying tension in me, an internal tension that I couldn't explain, but always felt. After making that choice to forgive in my own life, however, I felt as if a spring that had been wound tightly inside of me was released. That night when I went to bed, for the first time that I could remember, I felt totally at rest. I felt totally at peace, and didn't feel any tension at all.

We want to challenge you to forgive those who have hurt you. Find the freedom that can come only from forgiving those who have offended you. And then, once you have forgiven, (continue to walk in that forgiveness. That is the only way that you're going to experience intimacy with other people, and true intimacy with God.)

Ask your God to empower you. As Melanie said, nobody taught her this, but you have the benefit of now having been taught the importance of forgiving, and how to forgive. Ask the Lord to empower you, and then just *do it*. Take that step, and forgive. Then, from that day forward, stand on the moment that you forgave those who hurt you.

Stand on it, and walk in forgiveness.

(From this day forward, when people hurt you or commit an offense against you, you can own your feelings, acknowledge what they've done and how it's caused you to feel, and then forgive them right on the spot.)

Describing forgiveness and walking in forgiveness is a wonderful opportunity. I (Melanie) am thankful to be able to tell my story. It's not a pleasant story, and there was a time when I couldn't share it. I'm so thankful that I now feel free to do that, so that other people can read it, and can be comforted by knowing that there is freedom out there. There is a life outside of the walls that we build.

I (Steve) am so thankful that I've had the opportunity to speak with many people all over the world about this. We all share common hurts. It's a very ordinary thing. The Holy Spirit empowers us to release them, thereby releasing ourselves to be able to walk a free life. We are all able to have an emotionally and spiritually healthy life.

We pray that the Lord uses this book, that the Holy Spirit speaks to you, and that you are able to lay down all of the pain that you have suffered, no matter what your hurts are. Whether it's something horrible like Melanie's–and we know, there are so many that are even worse than her story–or whether they're things more like Steve has described, that may seem trivial to you. Hurts are hurts.

(Let them go. Allow the Holy Spirit to free you. Feel the joy of the Lord in your life again, and the joy of being with other people. Experience the intimacy that you can have, now that you're letting walls down.)

Just do it step by step. Walk it out day by day. Walk in the freedom that God is offering to you through this.

We pray that our Father will bless you and give you release. Let us leave you with a prayer, and ask for blessings in your life, as you forgive others:

Father, we pray in Jesus' name that your Holy Spirit will empower those now who have read this teaching, so that they will take the step of forgiveness towards those who have committed offenses against them. And then, having forgiven, we pray that you will empower them to walk in forgiveness and not take it back. As Melanie said, she could've taken it back so many times, but she never took it back on herself again.

We pray that that will be the story and experience of the one who is reading this book. We ask that your grace will empower and fill and equip them to forgive and walk in that, even as you've done for us.

We thank you. Thank you for what you've done in the lives of those who have read this. To your glory, Father. Amen.

Conclusion

If you have been impacted by this teaching on getting past the hurt and would like to let us know your story about how God has worked in your life and has enabled you to forgive those who have hurt you, we would love to hear from you. You can write us at:

gettingpasthehurt@gracewalk.org

Let us hear from you, and know your story. We want to know your experience because we want to celebrate with you what God has done in your life. Maybe your story could even be a part of future editions of this book, as we update and republish it.

We also invite you to visit our ministry website at **www.gracewalk.org.** On that site, you can find many other things to encourage you in your own grace walk, including radio programs, video teachings, and articles, plus links to Steve's other books, recorded resources, and his personal blog. We would also appreciate your positive reviews of this book on **amazon.com** or wherever you may have gotten it. Positive reviews will encourage others to read it.

Thanks again for investing your time with us. May God bless you and set you free as you forgive others, even as He has forgiven you, for Christ's sake.

About the Authors

Dr. Steve McVey is the President of Grace Walk, a ministry located in Atlanta, Georgia with satellite offices in Mexico, Canada, Pakistan, Australia, Argentina, and El Salvador. He is the author of the best-selling, *Grace Walk,* as well as eleven other books that can be seen at www.gracewalkresources.com. He is also the host of the daily "Grace Walk" radio program, airing across the United States.

Melanie has counseled ladies for forty years, as well spoken on the subject of grace for life's hurts. She and Steve live in the Atlanta area, and have four adult children and three grandchildren with a grandson due to arrive on Christmas Eve, 2013. They are still madly in love after 40 years of marriage.

Newest Books from Steve McVey

❖ ***Unlock Your Bible: The Key To Understanding and Applying the Scriptures in Your Life***

This book, available as an eBook or print paperback, will teach you a simple and practical way to read the Bible and understand it with ease. You'll discover how recognizing the difference between the Old and New Covenants are keys to understanding how to apply the Bible to your own life in ways that will make a difference. You'll also discover how to understand the hard things Jesus said, like how a person should pluck out his eye if he lusts. You will plainly see how to distinguish whether a verse you're reading was written *for* you or *to* you. The difference is huge.

❖ *When Wives Walk in Grace*

These short, easy-to-read chapters cover the most common challenges that wives face in marriage, and offer specific and practical advice on dealing with those challenges. You'll learn things like how to deal with verbal abuse, how to handle it if you feel your husband doesn't share your spiritual journey with you, how to move through arguments in a way that is helpful and not destructive, and how to balance your life when responsibilities seem to be more than you can handle. There are twenty-two chapters that deal with issues like these. You can take a look at the book or purchase it at Amazon.com.

Want To Join A Free Online Bible Study With Steve?

Every week, Steve posts a video teaching online that you can watch free at any time during the week. You can see it right on our home page at **www.gracewalk.org.**

One Last Thing ...

When you have finished reading this book, we would love it if you could return to Amazon.com to rate it and share your thoughts. They will even offer you an automatic feed to your Facebook and Twitter accounts. If you believe that your friends would get something valuable from reading *Getting Past the Hurt*, we would be honored if you'd post your thoughts. And if you feel particularly strongly about the contributions that this book makes in your own life, we'd be very grateful if you'd even post a review on **Amazon**. Positive reviews will move it higher in the search engine, and increase the likelihood that others will know about the book.

Would you do us that favor?

Thanks again. We appreciate you!

Made in the USA
San Bernardino, CA
14 March 2016